C000160866

Simply
Soup

Love Food™ is an imprint of Parragon Books Ltd

Parragon
Queen Street House
4 Queen Street
Bath BA1 1HE, UK

Copyright © Parragon Books Ltd 2007

Love Food™ and the accompanying heart device is a trade mark of Parragon Books Ltd.

All rights reserved. No part of this publication may be reproduced, stored in a retrieval system or transmitted, in any form or by any means, electronic, mechanical, photocopying, recording or otherwise, without the prior permission of the copyright holder.

ISBN 978-1-4075-1243-3

Printed in China

Photography by Mike Cooper
Food styling by Carole Handslip and Sumi Glass
Introduction by Pamela Gwyther

Notes for the reader
• This book uses metric and imperial measurements. Follow the same units of measurement throughout; do not mix imperial and metric.
• All spoon measurements are level: teaspoons are assumed to be 5 ml and tablespoons are assumed to be 15 ml.
• Unless otherwise stated, milk is assumed to be low fat and eggs are medium-size. The times given are an approximate guide only.
• Some recipes contain nuts. If you are allergic to nuts you should avoid using them and any products containing nuts.
• Recipes using raw or very lightly cooked eggs should be avoided by infants, the elderly, pregnant women, convalescents and anyone suffering from illness.

Front cover image: Minestrone (for recipe see page 13)

CONTENTS

Introduction

If you cook nothing else, you could live exceptionally well on the rich variety of soups you will find in this easy-to-use book.

In many ways, soup is simple. It is either thin, as in consommés, or thick, either puréed or left chunky. This means it can be eaten at different mealtime occasions – thinner broths make perfect starters or healthy snacks, while more robust soups incorporating fish, meat or vegetables can be a meal in themselves. For even more diversity, some soups can be served cold as well as hot – delicious on a hot summer's day.

There is a huge variety of ingredients and styles of soup, with many countries having their own traditional favourites – dishes that are firmly entrenched in that nation's culinary history; think of Spanish Gazpacho and Greek Avgolemono, Italian Minestrone and Ribollita, even Scottish Cullen Skink and Cock-a-leekie, to name but a few. Further east there are spicy Middle Eastern recipes and Indian lentil-based dhals. In the Far East, Thai flavours contrast with the blander Japanese Miso broth. Watch out for Bird's Nest Soup or Shark's Fin Soup when in China!

Soup-making is an exciting and challenging area of cookery. Don't be put off – all soups have three things in common, which help make them simple to understand and explore.

Firstly, soup is very easy to make. Almost all soups start with frying an onion with a tasty vegetable like leek or celery, to build a flavour base. You simply add an appropriate stock, together with the main ingredients of your choice, and cook for long enough to soften the textures and bring out the flavours. It really couldn't be simpler!

Secondly, home-made soup is healthy. You can guarantee the freshness and provenance of the raw ingredients, ensuring you are eating them in season and at the peak of their quality. There is usually very little fat involved and you can use the minimum amount of salt. This is why home-made soups are so much better for you than most commercially produced varieties.

Thirdly, soup is so convenient. It is ideal – fresh, or quickly defrosted from the freezer – for a quick meal or impromptu supper party at home, and it only needs a simple bowl for serving. It is easily portable too – just pack into a Thermos flask and you can enjoy a delicious cup of soup wherever and whenever you like.

Vegetable Stock

Makes: about 2 litres/3^{1}/$_{2}$ pints

Ingredients

2 tbsp sunflower oil

115 g/4 oz onion, finely chopped

40 g/1^{1}/$_{2}$ oz leek, finely chopped

115 g/4 oz carrots, finely chopped

4 celery sticks, finely chopped

85 g/3 oz fennel, finely chopped

1 small tomato, finely chopped

2.25 litres/4 pints water

1 bouquet garni

Heat the oil in a large saucepan. Add the onion and leek and cook over a low heat, stirring occasionally, for 5 minutes, until softened. Add the remaining vegetables, cover and cook for 10 minutes. Add the water and bouquet garni, bring to the boil and simmer for 20 minutes.

Strain the stock into a bowl, leave to cool, cover and store in the refrigerator. Use immediately or freeze in portions for up to 3 months.

Fish Stock

Makes: about 1.3 litres/2^{1}/$_{4}$ pints

Ingredients

650 g/1 lb 7 oz white fish heads, bones and trimmings, rinsed

1 onion, sliced

2 celery sticks, chopped

1 carrot, sliced

1 bay leaf

4 fresh parsley sprigs

4 black peppercorns

^{1}/$_{2}$ lemon, sliced

1.3 litres/2^{1}/$_{4}$ pints water

125 ml/4 fl oz dry white wine

Cut out and discard the gills from any fish heads, then place the heads, bones and trimmings in a saucepan. Add all the remaining ingredients and gradually bring to the boil, skimming off the scum that rises to the surface. Partially cover and simmer for 25 minutes.

Strain the stock without pressing down on the contents of the sieve. Leave to cool, cover and store in the refrigerator. Use immediately or freeze in portions for up to 3 months.

Chicken Stock

Makes: about 2.5 litres/4$^{1}/_{2}$ pints

Ingredients

1.3 kg/3 lb chicken wings and necks
2 onions, cut into wedges
4 litres/7 pints water
2 carrots, coarsely chopped
2 celery sticks, coarsely chopped
10 fresh parsley sprigs
4 fresh thyme sprigs
2 bay leaves
10 black peppercorns

Put the chicken wings and necks and the onions in a large saucepan and cook over a low heat, stirring frequently, until lightly browned.

Add the water and stir well to scrape off any sediment from the base of the pan. Gradually bring to the boil, skimming off the scum that rises to the surface. Add all the remaining ingredients, partially cover and simmer for 3 hours.

Strain the stock into a bowl, leave to cool, cover and store in the refrigerator. When cold, remove and discard the layer of fat from the surface. Use immediately or freeze in portions for up to 6 months.

Beef Stock

Makes: about 1.7 litres/3 pints

Ingredients

1 kg/2 lb 4 oz beef marrow bones, sawn into
    7.5-cm/3-inch pieces
650 g/1 lb 7 oz stewing steak in a single piece
2.8 litres/5 pints water
4 cloves
2 onions, halved
2 celery sticks, coarsely chopped
8 black peppercorns
1 bouquet garni

Place the bones in the base of a large saucepan and put the meat on top. Add the water and gradually bring to the boil, skimming off the scum that rises to the surface.

Press a clove into each onion half and add to the pan with the celery, peppercorns and bouquet garni. Partially cover and simmer for 3 hours. Remove the meat and simmer for 1 more hour.

Strain the stock into a bowl, leave to cool, cover and store in the refrigerator. When cold, remove and discard the layer of fat from the surface. Use immediately or freeze in portions for up to 6 months.

Classic Soups

In this chapter you will find all your old favourites, like Tomato Soup and Chicken Noodle Soup, along with some more sophisticated combinations, such as Clam & Corn Chowder and Bouillabaisse. There is nothing more welcoming to return home to than the aroma of freshly made soup and these familiar favourites are sure to be a hit with all the family.

Tomato Soup

Melt half the butter in a saucepan. Add the onion and cook over a low heat, stirring occasionally, for 5–6 minutes until softened. Add the tomatoes and bay leaf and cook, stirring occasionally, for 15 minutes, or until pulpy.

Meanwhile, melt the remaining butter in another saucepan. Add the flour and cook, stirring constantly, for 1 minute. Remove the pan from the heat and gradually stir in the milk. Return to the heat, season with salt and pepper and bring to the boil, stirring constantly. Continue to cook, stirring, until smooth and thickened.

When the tomatoes are pulpy, remove the pan from the heat. Discard the bay leaf and pour the tomato mixture into a blender or food processor. Process until smooth, then push through a sieve into a clean saucepan. Bring the tomato mixture to the boil, then gradually stir it into the milk mixture. Season to taste with salt and pepper. Ladle into warmed bowls, garnish with basil and serve immediately.

SERVES 4

55 g/2 oz butter

1 small onion, finely chopped

450 g/1 lb tomatoes, coarsely chopped

1 bay leaf

3 tbsp plain flour

600 ml/1 pint milk

salt and pepper

sprigs of fresh basil, to garnish

Minestrone

Heat the oil in a large saucepan. Add the garlic, onions and Parma ham and cook over a medium heat, stirring, for 3 minutes, until slightly softened. Add the red and orange peppers and the chopped tomatoes and cook for a further 2 minutes, stirring. Stir in the stock, then add the celery. Drain and add the borlotti beans along with the cabbage, peas and parsley. Season with salt and pepper. Bring to the boil, then lower the heat and simmer for 30 minutes.

Add the vermicelli to the pan. Cook for a further 10–12 minutes, or according to the instructions on the packet. Remove from the heat and ladle into serving bowls. Garnish with freshly grated Parmesan and serve immediately.

SERVES 4

2 tbsp olive oil

2 garlic cloves, chopped

2 red onions, chopped

75 g/2³/₄ oz Parma ham, sliced

1 red pepper, deseeded and chopped

1 orange pepper, deseeded and chopped

400 g/14 oz canned chopped tomatoes

1 litre/1³/₄ pints vegetable stock

1 celery stick, chopped

400 g/14 oz canned borlotti beans

100 g/3¹/₂ oz green leafy cabbage, shredded

75 g/2³/₄ oz frozen peas, defrosted

1 tbsp chopped fresh parsley

75 g/2³/₄ oz dried vermicelli

salt and pepper

freshly grated Parmesan cheese, to garnish

French Onion Soup

Heat the oil in a large, heavy-based saucepan over a medium-low heat, add the onions and cook, stirring occasionally, for 10 minutes, or until they are just beginning to brown. Stir in the chopped garlic, sugar and chopped thyme, then reduce the heat and cook, stirring occasionally, for 30 minutes, or until the onions are golden brown.

Sprinkle in the flour and cook, stirring constantly, for 1–2 minutes. Stir in the wine. Gradually stir in the stock and bring to the boil, skimming off any scum that rises to the surface, then reduce the heat and simmer for 45 minutes.

Meanwhile, preheat the grill to medium. Toast the bread on both sides under the grill, then rub the toast with the cut edges of the whole garlic clove.

Ladle the soup into 6 flameproof bowls set on a baking tray. Float a piece of toast in each bowl and divide the grated cheese between them. Place under the grill for 2–3 minutes, or until the cheese has just melted. Garnish with thyme sprigs and serve at once.

SERVES 6

3 tbsp olive oil

675 g/1 lb 8 oz onions, thinly sliced

4 garlic cloves, 3 chopped and
    1 peeled and halved

1 tsp sugar

2 tsp chopped fresh thyme, plus
    extra sprigs to garnish

2 tbsp plain flour

125 ml/4 fl oz dry white wine

2 litres/3$\frac{1}{2}$ pints vegetable stock

6 slices French bread

300 g/10$\frac{1}{2}$ oz Gruyère cheese,
    grated

Spiced Pumpkin Soup

Heat the oil in a saucepan over a medium heat. Add the onion and garlic and cook, stirring, for about 4 minutes, until slightly softened. Add the ginger, chilli, coriander, bay leaf and pumpkin and cook for another 3 minutes.

Pour in the stock and bring to the boil. Using a slotted spoon, skim any scum from the surface. Reduce the heat and simmer gently, stirring occasionally, for about 25 minutes, or until the pumpkin is tender. Remove from the heat, take out the bay leaf and leave to cool a little.

Transfer the soup to a food processor or blender and process until smooth (you may have to do this in batches). Return the mixture to the rinsed-out pan and season to taste with salt and pepper. Reheat gently, stirring. Remove from the heat, pour into 4 warmed soup bowls, garnish each one with a swirl of cream and serve.

SERVES 4

2 tbsp olive oil

1 onion, chopped

1 garlic clove, chopped

1 tbsp chopped fresh root ginger

1 small red chilli, deseeded and finely chopped

2 tbsp chopped fresh coriander

1 bay leaf

1 kg/2 lb 4 oz pumpkin, peeled, deseeded and diced

600 ml/1 pint vegetable stock

salt and pepper

single cream, to garnish

Split Pea & Ham Soup

Rinse the peas under cold running water. Put in a saucepan and cover generously with water. Bring to the boil and boil for 3 minutes, skimming off the scum from the surface. Drain the peas.

Heat the oil in a large saucepan over a medium heat. Add the onion and cook for 3–4 minutes, stirring occasionally, until just softened.

Add the carrot and celery and continue cooking for 2 minutes. Add the peas, pour over the stock and water and stir to combine.

Bring just to the boil and stir the ham into the soup. Add the thyme, marjoram and bay leaf. Reduce the heat, cover and cook gently for 1–1½ hours, until the ingredients are very soft. Remove the bay leaf.

Taste and adjust the seasoning. Ladle into warmed soup bowls and serve.

SERVES 6–8

500 g/1 lb 2 oz split green peas

1 tbsp olive oil

1 large onion, finely chopped

1 large carrot, finely chopped

1 celery sticks, finely chopped

1 litre/1³/₄ pints chicken or
    vegetable stock

1 litre/1³/₄ pints water

225 g/8 oz lean smoked ham,
    finely diced

¹/₄ tsp dried thyme

¹/₄ tsp dried marjoram

1 bay leaf

salt and pepper

Cream of Chicken Soup

Melt the butter in a large saucepan over a medium heat. Add the shallots and cook, stirring, for 3 minutes, until slightly softened. Add the leek and cook for a further 5 minutes, stirring. Add the chicken, stock and herbs, and season with salt and pepper. Bring to the boil, then lower the heat and simmer for 25 minutes, until the chicken is tender and cooked through. Remove from the heat and leave to cool for 10 minutes.

Transfer the soup to a food processor or blender and process until smooth (you may need to do this in batches). Return the soup to the rinsed-out pan and warm over a low heat for 5 minutes.

Stir in the cream and cook for a further 2 minutes, then remove from the heat and ladle into serving bowls. Garnish with sprigs of thyme and serve immediately.

SERVES 4

3 tbsp butter

4 shallots, chopped

1 leek, sliced

450 g/1 lb skinless chicken breasts, chopped

600 ml/1 pint chicken stock

1 tbsp chopped fresh parsley

1 tbsp chopped fresh thyme, plus extra sprigs to garnish

175 ml/6 fl oz double cream

salt and pepper

Chicken Noodle Soup

Place the chicken breasts in a large saucepan, add the water and bring to a simmer. Cook for 25–30 minutes. Skim any scum from the surface if necessary. Remove the chicken from the stock and keep warm.

While the stock is simmering, add the carrots and vermicelli and cook for 4–5 minutes.

Thinly slice or shred the chicken breasts and place in warmed serving dishes.

Season the soup to taste with salt and pepper and pour over the chicken. Serve at once garnished with the tarragon.

SERVES 4–6

2 skinless chicken breasts

1.2 litres/2 pints water or chicken stock

3 carrots, peeled and sliced into 5-mm/¼-inch slices

85 g/3 oz vermicelli (or other small noodles)

salt and pepper

fresh tarragon leaves, to garnish

Beef & Vegetable Soup

Place the pearl barley in a large saucepan. Pour over the stock and add the mixed herbs. Bring to the boil, cover and simmer gently over a low heat for 10 minutes.

Meanwhile, trim any fat from the beef and cut the meat into thin strips.

With a slotted spoon, skim away any scum that has risen to the top of the stock.

Add the beef, carrot, leek, onion and celery to the pan. Bring back to the boil, cover and simmer for about 1 hour or until the pearl barley, beef and vegetables are just tender.

With a flat ladle, skim away any remaining scum that has risen to the top of the soup. Blot the surface with absorbent kitchen paper to remove any fat. Adjust the seasoning according to taste.

Ladle the soup into warmed bowls, garnish with chopped parsley and serve hot.

SERVES 4

55 g/2 oz pearl barley

1.2 litres/2 pints beef stock

1 tsp dried mixed herbs

225 g/8 oz lean rump or sirloin beef

1 large carrot, diced

1 leek, shredded

1 medium onion, chopped

2 celery sticks, sliced

salt and pepper

2 tbsp chopped fresh parsley, to garnish

Clam & Corn Chowder

If using fresh clams, wash under cold running water. Discard any with broken shells or any that refuse to close when tapped. Put the clams into a heavy-based saucepan with the wine. Cover tightly, set over a medium-high heat and cook for 2–4 minutes, or until they open, shaking the pan occasionally. Discard any that remain closed. Remove the clams from the shells and strain the cooking liquid through a very fine mesh sieve; reserve both. If using canned clams, drain and rinse well.

Melt the butter in a large saucepan over a medium-low heat. Add the onion and carrot and cook for 3–4 minutes, stirring frequently, until the onion is softened. Stir in the flour and continue cooking for 2 minutes.

Slowly add about half the stock and stir well, scraping the bottom of the pan to mix in the flour. Pour in the remaining stock and the reserved clam cooking liquid, or the water if using canned clams, and bring just to the boil, stirring.

Add the potatoes, sweetcorn and milk and stir to combine. Reduce the heat and simmer gently, partially covered, for about 20 minutes, stirring occasionally, until all the vegetables are tender.

Chop the clams, if large. Stir in the clams and continue cooking for about 5 minutes until heated through. Taste and adjust the seasoning, if needed.

Ladle the soup into bowls and sprinkle with parsley.

SERVES 4

750 g/1 lb 10 oz clams, or 280 g/ 10 oz canned clams

2 tbsp dry white wine (if using fresh clams)

4 tsp butter

1 large onion, finely chopped

1 small carrot, finely diced

3 tbsp plain flour

300 ml/10 fl oz fish stock

200 ml/7 fl oz water (if using canned clams)

450 g/1 lb potatoes, diced

125 g/4 oz sweetcorn, thawed if frozen

450 ml/16 fl oz full-fat milk

salt and pepper

chopped fresh parsley, to garnish

Bouillabaisse

Heat the oil in a large pan over a medium heat. Add the garlic and onions and cook, stirring, for 3 minutes. Stir in the tomatoes, stock, wine, bay leaf, saffron and herbs. Bring to the boil, reduce the heat, cover and simmer for 30 minutes.

Meanwhile, soak the mussels in lightly salted water for 10 minutes. Scrub the shells under cold running water and pull off any beards. Discard any mussels with broken shells or any that refuse to close when tapped. Put the rest into a large pan with a little water, bring to the boil and cook over a high heat for 4 minutes. Remove from the heat and discard any that remain closed.

When the tomato mixture is cooked, rinse the fish fillets, pat dry and cut into chunks. Add to the pan and simmer for 5 minutes. Add the mussels, prawns and scallops and season with salt and pepper. Cook for 3 minutes, until the fish is cooked through. Remove from the heat, discard the bay leaf and ladle into serving bowls.

SERVES 4

100 ml/$3^1/_2$ fl oz olive oil

3 garlic cloves, chopped

2 onions, chopped

2 tomatoes, deseeded and chopped

700 ml/$1^1/_4$ pints fish stock

400 ml/14 fl oz white wine

1 bay leaf

pinch of saffron threads

2 tbsp chopped fresh basil

2 tbsp chopped fresh parsley

200 g/7 oz live mussels

250 g/9 oz snapper or monkfish fillets

250 g/9 oz haddock fillets, skinned

200 g/7 oz prawns, peeled and deveined

100 g/$3^1/_2$ oz scallops

salt and pepper

Hearty Soups

These nourishing and satisfying bowlfuls are ideal comfort food on a cold winter's day. Try Ribollita or Mushroom & Barley Soup – both are meals in themselves, but those with especially large appetites can serve them with chunks of fresh bread. These soups are perfect for filling the gap and keeping you going, however hectic your day might be.

Roasted Mediterranean Vegetable Soup

Preheat the oven to 190°C/375°F/Gas Mark 5.

Brush a large shallow baking dish with olive oil. Laying them cut-side down, arrange the tomatoes, peppers, courgettes and aubergine in one layer (use two dishes, if necessary). Tuck the garlic cloves and onion pieces into the gaps and drizzle the vegetables with the remaining olive oil. Season lightly with salt and pepper and sprinkle with the thyme.

Place in the preheated oven and bake, uncovered, for 30–35 minutes, or until soft and browned around the edges. Leave to cool, then scrape out the aubergine flesh and remove the skin from the peppers.

Working in batches, put the aubergine and pepper flesh, together with the tomatoes, courgettes, garlic and onion, into a food processor and chop to the consistency of salsa or pickle; do not purée. Alternatively, place in a bowl and chop together with a knife.

Combine the stock and chopped vegetable mixture in a saucepan and simmer over a medium heat for 20–30 minutes, until all the vegetables are tender and the flavours have completely blended.

Stir in the cream and simmer over a low heat for about 5 minutes, stirring occasionally until hot. Taste and adjust the seasoning, if necessary. Ladle the soup into warmed bowls, garnish with basil and serve.

SERVES 6

3 tbsp olive oil

700 g/1 lb 9 oz ripe tomatoes, skinned, cored and halved

3 large yellow peppers, deseeded and halved

3 courgettes, halved lengthways

1 small aubergine, halved lengthways

4 garlic cloves, halved

2 onions, cut into eighths

pinch of dried thyme

1 litre/$1^3/_4$ pints chicken or vegetable stock

120 ml/4 fl oz single cream

salt and pepper

shredded basil leaves, to garnish

Ribollita

Heat the oil in a large saucepan and cook the onions, carrots and celery for 10–15 minutes, stirring frequently. Add the garlic, thyme and salt and pepper to taste. Continue to cook for a further 1–2 minutes, until the vegetables are golden and caramelized.

Add the cannellini beans to the pan and pour in the tomatoes. Add enough of the water to cover the vegetables.

Bring to the boil and simmer for 20 minutes. Add the parsley and cavolo nero and cook for a further 5 minutes.

Stir in the bread and add a little more water, if needed. The soup should be thick.

Taste and adjust the seasoning, if necessary. Ladle into warmed serving bowls and serve hot, drizzled with extra virgin olive oil.

SERVES 4

3 tbsp olive oil

2 medium red onions, coarsely chopped

3 carrots, sliced

3 celery sticks, coarsely chopped

3 garlic cloves, chopped

1 tbsp chopped fresh thyme

400 g/14 oz canned cannellini beans, drained and rinsed

400 g/14 oz canned chopped tomatoes

600 ml/1 pint water or vegetable stock

2 tbsp chopped fresh parsley

500 g/1 lb 2 oz cavolo nero or Savoy cabbage, trimmed and sliced

1 small day-old ciabatta loaf, torn into small pieces

salt and pepper

extra virgin olive oil, to serve

Mushroom & Barley Soup

Rinse the pearl barley and drain. Bring 450 ml/16 fl oz of the stock to the boil in a small saucepan. Add the bay leaf and, if the stock is unsalted, add a large pinch of salt. Stir in the pearl barley, reduce the heat, cover and simmer for 40 minutes.

Melt the butter in a large frying pan over a medium heat. Add the mushrooms and season with salt and pepper. Cook for about 8 minutes until they are golden brown, stirring occasionally at first, then more often after they start to colour. Remove the mushrooms from the heat.

Heat the oil in a large saucepan over a medium heat and add the onion and carrots. Cover and cook for about 3 minutes, stirring frequently, until the onion is softened.

Add the remaining stock and bring to the boil. Stir in the barley with its cooking liquid and add the mushrooms. Reduce the heat, cover and simmer gently for about 20 minutes, or until the carrots are tender, stirring occasionally.

Stir in the tarragon and parsley. Taste and adjust the seasoning, if necessary. Ladle into warmed bowls, garnish with fresh parsley and tarragon and serve.

SERVES 4

55 g/2 oz pearl barley

1.5 litres/$2^3/_4$ pints chicken or vegetable stock

1 bay leaf

1 tbsp butter

350 g/12 oz mushrooms, thinly sliced

1 tsp olive oil

1 onion, finely chopped

2 carrots, thinly sliced

1 tbsp chopped fresh tarragon, plus extra to garnish

1 tbsp chopped fresh parsley, plus extra to garnish

salt and pepper

Kidney Bean, Pumpkin & Tomato Soup

Pick over the beans, cover generously with cold water and leave to soak for 6 hours or overnight. Drain the beans, put in a saucepan and add enough cold water to cover by 5 cm/2 inches. Bring to the boil and boil for 10 minutes. Drain and rinse well.

Heat the oil in a large saucepan over a medium heat. Add the onions, cover and cook for 3–4 minutes, until they are just softened, stirring occasionally. Add the garlic, celery and carrot, and continue cooking for 2 minutes.

Add the water, drained beans, tomato purée, thyme, oregano, cumin and bay leaf. When the mixture begins to bubble, reduce the heat to low. Cover and simmer gently for 1 hour, stirring occasionally.

Stir in the tomatoes, pumpkin and chilli purée and continue simmering for a further hour, or until the beans and pumpkin are tender, stirring from time to time.

Season to taste with salt and pepper and stir in a little more chilli purée, if liked. Ladle the soup into bowls, garnish with coriander and serve.

SERVES 4–6

250 g/9 oz dried kidney beans

1 tbsp olive oil

2 onions, finely chopped

4 garlic cloves, finely chopped

1 celery stick, thinly sliced

1 carrot, halved and thinly sliced

1.2 litres/2 pints water

2 tsp tomato purée

$1/8$ tsp dried thyme

$1/8$ tsp dried oregano

$1/8$ tsp ground cumin

1 bay leaf

400 g/14 oz canned chopped
  tomatoes

250 g/9 oz peeled pumpkin flesh,
  diced

$1/4$ tsp chilli purée, or to taste

salt and pepper

fresh coriander leaves, to garnish

Chicken Gumbo Soup

Heat the oil in a large heavy-based saucepan over a medium-low heat and stir in the flour. Cook for about 15 minutes, stirring occasionally, until the mixture is a rich golden brown.

Add the onion, green pepper and celery and continue cooking for about 10 minutes until the onion softens.

Slowly pour in the stock and bring to the boil, stirring well and scraping the bottom of the pan to mix in the flour. Remove the pan from the heat.

Add the tomatoes and garlic. Stir in the okra and rice and season to taste with salt and pepper. Reduce the heat, cover and simmer for 20 minutes, or until the okra is tender.

Add the chicken and sausage and continue simmering for about 10 minutes. Taste and adjust the seasoning, if necessary, and ladle into warmed bowls to serve.

SERVES 6

2 tbsp olive oil

4 tbsp plain flour

1 onion, finely chopped

1 small green pepper, deseeded and finely chopped

1 stick celery, finely chopped

1.2 litres/2 pints chicken stock

400 g/14 oz canned chopped tomatoes

3 garlic cloves, finely chopped or crushed

125 g/4^{1}/$_{2}$ oz okra, stems removed, cut into 5-mm/^{1}/$_{4}$-inch thick slices

50 g/1^{3}/$_{4}$ oz white rice

200 g/7 oz cooked chicken, cubed

115 g/4 oz cooked garlic sausage, sliced or cubed

salt and pepper

Chicken & Potato Soup with Bacon

Melt the butter in a large saucepan over a medium heat. Add the garlic and onion and cook, stirring, for 3 minutes, until slightly softened. Add the chopped bacon and leeks and cook for a further 3 minutes, stirring.

In a bowl, mix the flour with enough stock to make a smooth paste, then stir it into the pan. Cook, stirring, for 2 minutes. Pour in the remaining stock, then add the potatoes and chicken. Season with salt and pepper. Bring to the boil, then lower the heat and simmer for 25 minutes, until the chicken and potatoes are tender and cooked through.

Stir in the cream and cook for a further 2 minutes, then remove from the heat and ladle into serving bowls. Garnish with the grilled bacon and flat-leaf parsley, and serve immediately.

SERVES 4

1 tbsp butter

2 garlic cloves, chopped

1 onion, sliced

250 g/9 oz smoked lean back bacon, chopped

2 large leeks, sliced

2 tbsp plain flour

1 litre/$1^3/_4$ pints chicken stock

800 g/1 lb 12 oz potatoes, chopped

200 g/7 oz skinless chicken breast, chopped

4 tbsp double cream

salt and pepper

grilled bacon and sprigs of fresh flat-leaf parsley, to garnish

Sausage & Red Cabbage Soup

Heat the oil in a large saucepan. Add the garlic and onion and cook over a medium heat, stirring, for 3 minutes, until slightly softened. Add the leek and cook for a further 3 minutes, stirring.

In a bowl, mix the cornflour with enough stock to make a smooth paste, then stir it into the pan. Cook, stirring, for 2 minutes. Stir in the remaining stock, then add the potatoes and sausages. Season with salt and pepper. Bring to the boil, then lower the heat and simmer for 25 minutes.

Add the red cabbage and beans and cook for 10 minutes, then stir in the cream and cook for a further 5 minutes. Remove from the heat and ladle into serving bowls. Garnish with ground paprika and serve immediately.

SERVES 4

2 tbsp olive oil

1 garlic clove, chopped

1 large onion, chopped

1 large leek, sliced

2 tbsp cornflour

1 litre/$1^3/_4$ pints vegetable stock

450 g/1 lb potatoes, sliced

200 g/7 oz skinless sausages, sliced

150 g/$5^1/_2$ oz red cabbage, chopped

200 g/7 oz canned black-eye
    beans, drained

125 ml/4 fl oz double cream

salt and pepper

ground paprika, to garnish

Scotch Broth

Heat the vegetable oil in a large, heavy-based saucepan and add the pieces of lamb, turning them to seal and brown on both sides. Lift the lamb out of the pan and set aside until required.

Add the onion, carrots and leeks to the saucepan and cook gently for about 3 minutes.

Return the lamb to the saucepan and add the vegetable stock, bay leaf, parsley and pearl barley. Bring the mixture to the boil, then reduce the heat. Cover and simmer for 1½–2 hours.

Discard the parsley sprigs. Lift the pieces of lamb from the broth and allow them to cool slightly. Remove the bones and any fat and chop the meat. Return the lamb to the broth and reheat gently. Season to taste with salt and pepper.

It is advisable to prepare this soup a day ahead, then leave it to cool, cover and refrigerate overnight. When ready to serve, remove and discard the layer of fat from the surface and reheat the soup gently. Ladle into warmed bowls and serve immediately.

SERVES 4

1 tbsp vegetable oil

500 g/1 lb 2 oz lean neck of lamb

1 large onion, sliced

2 carrots, sliced

2 leeks, sliced

1 litre/1¾ pints vegetable stock

1 bay leaf

sprigs of fresh parsley

55 g/2 oz pearl barley

salt and pepper

Beef & Bean Soup

Heat the oil in a large saucepan over a medium heat. Add the onion and garlic and cook, stirring frequently, for 5 minutes, or until softened. Add the pepper and carrots and cook for a further 5 minutes.

Meanwhile, drain the beans, reserving the liquid from the can. Place two thirds of the beans, reserving the remaining third, in a food processor or blender with the bean liquid and process until smooth.

Add the mince to the saucepan and cook until well browned, stirring constantly to break up any lumps. Add the spices and cook, stirring, for 2 minutes. Add the cabbage, tomatoes, stock and puréed beans and season to taste with salt and pepper. Bring to the boil, then reduce the heat, cover and simmer for 15 minutes, or until the vegetables are tender.

Stir in the remaining beans, cover and simmer for a further 5 minutes. Ladle the soup into warmed soup bowls and serve.

SERVES 4

2 tbsp vegetable oil

1 large onion, finely chopped

2 garlic cloves, finely chopped

1 green pepper, deseeded and sliced

2 carrots, sliced

400 g/14 oz canned black-eye beans

225 g/8 oz fresh beef mince

1 tsp each ground cumin, chilli powder and paprika

$^1/_4$ cabbage, sliced

225 g/8 oz tomatoes, peeled and chopped

600 ml/1 pint beef stock

salt and pepper

Seafood Chowder

Discard any mussels with broken shells or any that refuse to close when tapped. Rinse, and pull off any beards. Put the mussels in a large heavy-based saucepan. Cover tightly and cook over a high heat for about 4 minutes, or until the mussels open, shaking the pan occasionally. Discard any that remain closed. When they are cool enough to handle, remove the mussels from the shells, adding any additional juices to the cooking liquid. Strain the cooking liquid through a muslin-lined sieve and reserve.

Put the flour in a mixing bowl and very slowly whisk in enough of the stock to make a thick paste. Whisk in a little more stock to make a smooth liquid.

Melt the butter in a heavy-based saucepan over a medium-low heat. Add the onion, cover and cook for about 5 minutes, stirring frequently, until it softens.

Add the remaining fish stock and bring to the boil. Slowly whisk in the flour mixture until well combined and bring back to the boil, whisking constantly. Add the mussel cooking liquid. Season with salt, if needed, and pepper. Reduce the heat and simmer, partially covered, for 15 minutes.

Add the fish and mussels and continue simmering, stirring occasionally, for about 5 minutes, or until the fish is cooked and begins to flake.

Stir in the prawns and cream. Taste and adjust the seasoning. Simmer for a few minutes longer to heat through. Ladle into warmed bowls, sprinkle with dill and serve.

SERVES 6

1 kg/2 lb 4 oz live mussels

4 tbsp plain flour

1.5 litres/$2^3/_4$ pints fish stock

1 tbsp butter

1 large onion, finely chopped

350 g/12 oz skinless white fish fillets, such as cod, sole or haddock

200 g/7 oz cooked or raw peeled prawns

300 ml/10 fl oz whipping cream or double cream

salt and pepper

snipped fresh dill, to garnish

Refreshing Soups

The recipes in this section are light in texture and fresh in taste, making them perfect for the summer months or as an elegant starter. Try Chilled Avocado Soup on a hot day, or Wonton Soup when it's a little cooler. Remember that the fresher the ingredients, the fuller the flavour of the soup — make sure that you use fresh seasonal produce for perfect results.

Vichyssoise

Trim the leeks and remove most of the green part. Slice the white part of the leeks very finely.

Melt the butter in a saucepan. Add the leeks and onion and fry, stirring occasionally, for about 5 minutes without browning.

Add the potatoes, stock, lemon juice, nutmeg, coriander and bay leaf to the pan, season to taste with salt and pepper and bring to the boil. Cover and simmer for about 30 minutes, until all the vegetables are very soft.

Cool the soup a little, remove and discard the bay leaf and then press through a strainer or process in a food processor or blender until smooth. Pour into a clean pan.

Blend the egg yolk into the cream, add a little of the soup to the mixture and then whisk it all back into the soup and reheat gently, without boiling. Adjust the seasoning to taste. Cool and then chill thoroughly in the refrigerator.

Serve the soup sprinkled with freshly snipped chives.

SERVES 6

3 large leeks

40 g/$1^1/_2$ oz butter or margarine

1 onion, thinly sliced

500 g/1 lb 2 oz potatoes, chopped

850 ml/$1^1/_2$ pints vegetable stock

2 tsp lemon juice

pinch of ground nutmeg

$^1/_4$ tsp ground coriander

1 bay leaf

1 egg yolk

150 ml/5 fl oz single cream

salt and pepper

freshly snipped chives, to garnish

Chilled Avocado Soup

Put the lemon juice into a blender or food processor. Halve the avocados and remove the stones. Scoop out the flesh and chop coarsely.

Place the avocado flesh, chives, parsley, stock, cream and Worcestershire sauce in the blender and process to a smooth purée.

Transfer to a bowl and season to taste with salt and pepper. Cover the bowl tightly with clingfilm and chill in the refrigerator for at least 30 minutes.

To serve, stir, then ladle into chilled soup bowls and garnish with a swirl of cream and a sprinkling of snipped chives.

SERVES 4

1 tbsp lemon juice

2 avocados

1 tbsp snipped fresh chives,
    plus extra to garnish

1 tbsp chopped fresh flat-leaf
    parsley

425 ml/15 fl oz cold chicken stock

300 ml/10 fl oz single cream,
    plus extra to garnish

dash of Worcestershire sauce

salt and pepper

Miso Soup

Put the water in a large pan with the dashi granules and bring to the boil. Add the tofu and mushrooms, reduce the heat, and let simmer for 3 minutes.

Stir in the miso paste and let simmer gently, stirring, until it has dissolved.

Add the spring onions and serve immediately. If you leave the soup, the miso will settle, so give the soup a thorough stir before serving to recombine.

SERVES 4

1 litre/$1^3/_4$ pints water

2 tsp dashi granules

175 g/6 oz silken tofu, drained and cut into small cubes

4 shiitake mushrooms, finely sliced

4 tbsp miso paste

2 spring onions, chopped

Gazpacho

Tear the bread into pieces and place in a food processor or blender. Process briefly to make breadcrumbs and transfer to a large bowl. Add the tomatoes, garlic, red peppers, cucumber, oil, vinegar and tomato purée. Mix well.

Working in batches, place the tomato mixture with an equal volume of the measured water in the food processor or blender and process to a purée. Transfer to another bowl. When all the tomato mixture and water have been blended together, stir well and season to taste with salt and pepper. Cover with clingfilm and chill in the refrigerator for at least 2 hours, but no longer than 12 hours.

When ready to serve, pour the soup into chilled serving bowls and float an ice cube in each bowl.

SERVES 4

250 g/9 oz white bread slices, crusts removed

700 g/1 lb 9 oz tomatoes, peeled and chopped

3 garlic cloves, coarsely chopped

2 red peppers, deseeded and coarsely chopped

1 cucumber, peeled, deseeded and chopped

5 tbsp extra virgin olive oil

5 tbsp red wine vinegar

1 tbsp tomato purée

850 ml/1^1/$_2$ pints water

salt and pepper

4 ice cubes, to serve

Chilled Borscht

Put the cabbage in a pan and cover generously with cold water. Bring to the boil, boil for 3 minutes, then drain.

Heat the oil in a large saucepan over a medium-low heat. Add the onion and leek, cover and cook for about 5 minutes, stirring occasionally, until the vegetables begin to soften.

Add the tomatoes, water, carrot, parsnip, beetroot and bay leaf. Stir in the blanched cabbage and add a large pinch of salt. Bring to the boil, reduce the heat and simmer for about 1¼ hours until all the vegetables are tender. Remove and discard the bay leaf.

Allow the soup to cool slightly, then transfer to a food processor or blender and process until smooth, working in batches if necessary. If using a food processor, strain off the cooking liquid and reserve. Purée the soup solids with enough cooking liquid to moisten them, then combine with the reserved liquid.

Pour the soup into a large container and stir in the tomato juice. Allow to cool and refrigerate until cold.

Add the dill and stir. Thin the soup with more tomato juice or water, if liked. Season to taste with salt and pepper and, if you prefer it less sweet, add a few drops of lemon juice. Ladle into chilled soup bowls, and top each with a spoonful of soured cream and a sprig of dill.

SERVES 4–6

¹/₄ medium cabbage, cored and coarsely chopped

1 tbsp vegetable oil

1 onion, finely chopped

1 leek, halved lengthways and sliced

400 g / 14 oz canned peeled tomatoes in juice

1.2 litres / 2 pints water, plus extra if needed

1 carrot, thinly sliced

1 small parsnip, finely chopped

3 beetroot (raw or cooked), peeled and cubed

1 bay leaf

350 ml / 12 fl oz tomato juice, plus extra if needed

2–3 tbsp chopped fresh dill, plus extra sprigs to garnish

fresh lemon juice (optional)

salt and pepper

soured cream or yogurt, to garnish

Lemon Veal Soup with Mushrooms

Put the veal in a large saucepan and add the stock. Bring just to the boil and skim off any scum that rises to the surface.

Add the onion, carrots, garlic, lemon rind and bay leaf. Season with salt and pepper. Reduce the heat and simmer, partially covered, for about 45 minutes, stirring occasionally, until the veal is very tender.

Remove the veal and carrots with a slotted spoon and reserve, covered. Strain the stock into a clean saucepan. Discard the onion and garlic, lemon rind and bay leaf.

Melt the butter in a frying pan over a medium-high heat. Add the mushrooms, season, and fry gently until lightly golden. Reserve with the veal and carrots.

Mix together the cornflour and cream. Bring the stock just to the boil and whisk in the cream mixture. Boil very gently for 2–3 minutes until it thickens, whisking almost constantly.

Add the reserved meat and vegetables to the soup and simmer over a low heat for about 5 minutes until heated through. Taste and adjust the seasoning, adding nutmeg and a squeeze of lemon juice, if using. Stir in the parsley, then ladle into warmed bowls and serve.

SERVES 4

350 g/12 oz boneless veal, cut into
   1-cm/^{1}/$_2$-inch pieces
1 litre/1^3/$_4$ pints chicken stock
1 onion, quartered
2 carrots, thinly sliced
2 garlic cloves, halved
1 pared strip lemon rind
1 bay leaf
1 tbsp butter
350 g/12 oz small button
   mushrooms, quartered
4 tbsp cornflour
125 ml/4 fl oz double cream
freshly grated nutmeg
fresh lemon juice, to taste (optional)
1–2 tbsp chopped fresh parsley
salt and pepper

Wonton Soup

For the wonton filling, mix together the pork, prawns, ginger, soy sauce, rice wine, spring onion, sugar, pepper and sesame oil, and stir well until the texture is thick and pasty. Set aside for at least 20 minutes.

To make the wontons, place a teaspoon of the filling at the centre of a wrapper. Brush the edges with a little egg white. Bring the opposite points towards each other and press the edges together, creating a flower-like shape. Repeat with the remaining wrappers and filling.

To make the soup, bring the stock to the boil and add the salt and the pepper (omit the salt if using a stock that is already salty). Boil the wontons in the stock for about 5 minutes until the wrappers begin to wrinkle around the filling.

To serve, put the spring onion in individual bowls, spoon in the wontons and soup and top with the coriander.

SERVES 6–8

2 litres/$3^1/_2$ pints chicken stock

2 tsp salt

$^1/_2$ tsp white pepper

2 tbsp finely chopped spring onion, to serve

1 tbsp chopped fresh coriander leaves, to serve

wontons

175 g/6 oz minced pork, not too lean

225 g/8 oz raw prawns, peeled, deveined and chopped

$^1/_2$ tsp finely chopped fresh root ginger

1 tbsp light soy sauce

1 tbsp Shaoxing rice wine

2 tsp finely chopped spring onion

pinch of sugar

pinch of white pepper

dash of sesame oil

30 square wonton wrappers

1 egg white, lightly beaten

Consommé

Put the stock and minced beef in a saucepan and leave for 1 hour. Add the tomatoes, carrots, onion, celery, turnip, if using, bouquet garni, 2 of the egg whites, the crushed shells of 2 of the eggs and plenty of seasoning. Bring to almost boiling point, whisking hard all the time with a flat whisk.

Cover and simmer for 1 hour, taking care not to allow the layer of froth on top of the soup to break.

Pour the soup through a fine cloth into another pan, keeping the froth back until the last moment. Then pour the soup through the cloth again into a clean pan. Discard the cloth and its contents. The resulting liquid should be clear.

If the soup is not quite clear, return it to the pan with another egg white and the crushed shells of 2 more eggs. Repeat the whisking process as before and then boil for 10 minutes; strain again.

Add the sherry, if using, to the soup and reheat gently. Place the garnish in the warmed soup bowls and carefully pour in the soup. Serve immediately.

SERVES 4–6

1.25 litres/$2^1/_4$ pints beef stock

225 g/8 oz fresh extra lean beef mince

2 tomatoes, skinned, deseeded and chopped

2 large carrots, chopped

1 large onion, chopped

2 celery sticks, chopped

1 turnip, chopped (optional)

1 bouquet garni

2–3 egg whites

shells of 2–4 eggs, crushed

1–2 tbsp sherry (optional)

salt and pepper

julienne strips of raw carrot, turnip, celery or celeriac, to garnish

Seared Scallops in Garlic Broth

Combine the garlic cloves, celery, carrot, onion, peppercorns, parsley stems and water in a saucepan with a good pinch of salt. Bring to the boil, reduce the heat and simmer, partially covered, for 30–45 minutes.

Strain the stock into a clean saucepan. Taste and adjust the seasoning, and keep hot.

If using sea scallops, slice in half horizontally to form 2 thinner rounds from each. (If the scallops are very large, slice them into 3 rounds.) Sprinkle with salt and pepper.

Heat the oil in a frying pan over a medium-high heat and cook the scallops on one side for 1–2 minutes, until lightly browned and the flesh becomes opaque.

Divide the scallops among 4 warmed shallow bowls, arranging them browned-side up. Ladle the soup over the scallops, then float a few coriander leaves on top. Serve immediately.

SERVES 4

1 large garlic bulb (about 100 g/ $3^1/_2$ oz), separated into unpeeled cloves

1 celery stick, chopped

1 carrot, chopped

1 onion, chopped

10 peppercorns

5–6 parsley stems

1.2 litres/2 pints water

225 g/8 oz large sea scallops

1 tbsp oil

salt and pepper

fresh coriander leaves, to garnish

Cold Cucumber & Smoked Salmon Soup

Heat the oil in a large saucepan over a medium heat. Add the onion and cook for about 3 minutes, until it begins to soften.

Add the cucumber, potato, celery and stock, along with a large pinch of salt, if using unsalted stock. Bring to the boil, reduce the heat, cover and cook gently for about 20 minutes until the vegetables are tender.

Allow the soup to cool slightly, then transfer to a food processor or blender, working in batches if necessary. Purée the soup until smooth. If using a food processor, strain off the cooking liquid and reserve it. Purée the soup solids with enough cooking liquid to moisten them, then combine with the remaining liquid.

Transfer the puréed soup to a large container. Cover and refrigerate until cold.

Stir the cream, salmon and chives into the soup. If time permits, chill for at least 1 hour to allow the flavours to blend. Taste and adjust the seasoning, adding salt, if needed, and pepper. Ladle into chilled bowls and serve.

SERVES 4

2 tsp oil

1 large onion, finely chopped

1 large cucumber, peeled, deseeded and sliced

1 small potato, diced

1 celery stick, finely chopped

1 litre/$1^3/_4$ pints chicken or vegetable stock

150 ml/5 fl oz double cream

150 g/$5^1/_2$ oz smoked salmon, finely diced

2 tbsp snipped fresh chives

salt and pepper

Spicy Soups

This chapter explores the world of spice with an exciting selection of internationally inspired dishes. The recipes range in heat from the warming Mushroom & Ginger Soup to the carefully balanced Hot & Sour Soup with Tofu, and from the fiery Pork Chilli Soup to the delicately spiced Thai Chicken-Coconut Soup. All are guaranteed to spice up and add excitement to your mealtimes.

Hot & Sour Soup with Tofu

Put the lime rind, garlic and ginger into a large saucepan with the stock and bring to the boil. Reduce the heat and simmer for 5 minutes. Remove the lime rind, garlic and ginger with a slotted spoon and discard.

Meanwhile, heat the vegetable oil in a large frying pan over a high heat, add the tofu and cook, turning frequently, until golden. Remove from the pan and drain on kitchen paper.

Add the noodles, mushrooms and chilli to the stock and simmer for 3 minutes. Add the tofu, spring onions, soy sauce, lime juice, rice wine and sesame oil and briefly heat through.

Divide the soup among 4 warmed bowls, scatter the coriander over and serve immediately.

SERVES 4

3 strips of rind and juice of 1 lime

2 garlic cloves, peeled

2 slices fresh root ginger

1 litre/$1^3/_4$ pints chicken stock

1 tbsp vegetable oil

150 g/$5^1/_2$ oz firm tofu (drained weight), cubed

200 g/7 oz dried fine egg noodles

100 g/$3^1/_2$ oz shiitake mushrooms, sliced

1 fresh red chilli, deseeded and sliced

4 spring onions, sliced

1 tsp soy sauce

1 tsp Chinese rice wine

1 tsp sesame oil

chopped fresh coriander, to garnish

Mushroom & Ginger Soup

Soak the dried Chinese mushrooms for at least 30 minutes in 300 ml/10 fl oz of the hot stock. Drain the mushrooms and reserve the stock. Remove the stalks of the mushrooms and discard. Slice the caps and reserve. Cook the noodles for 2–3 minutes in boiling water, then drain and rinse. Reserve until required.

Heat the sunflower oil in a preheated wok or large, heavy-based frying pan over a high heat. Add the garlic and ginger, stir and add the mushrooms. Stir over a high heat for 2 minutes.

Add the remaining vegetable stock with the reserved stock and bring to the boil. Add the mushroom ketchup and soy sauce. Stir in the beansprouts and cook until tender.

Place some noodles in each soup bowl and ladle the soup on top. Garnish with fresh coriander sprigs and serve immediately.

SERVES 4

15 g/^{1}/$_2$ oz dried Chinese mushrooms or 125 g/4^1/$_2$ oz field or chestnut mushrooms

1 litre/1^3/$_4$ pints hot vegetable stock

125 g/4^1/$_2$ oz fine egg noodles

2 tsp sunflower oil

3 garlic cloves, crushed

2.5-cm/1-inch piece fresh root ginger, finely shredded

^{1}/$_2$ tsp mushroom ketchup

1 tsp light soy sauce

125 g/4^1/$_2$ oz beansprouts

fresh coriander sprigs, to garnish

Thai Chicken-Coconut Soup

Soak the dried noodles in a large bowl with enough lukewarm water to cover for 20 minutes, until soft. Alternatively, cook according to the packet instructions. Drain well and set aside.

Meanwhile, bring the stock to the boil in a large saucepan over a high heat. Lower the heat, add the lemon grass, ginger, lime leaves and chilli and simmer for 5 minutes. Add the chicken and continue simmering for a further 3 minutes, or until cooked. Stir in the coconut cream, nam pla and 1 tablespoon lime juice and continue simmering for 3 minutes. Add the beansprouts and spring onions and simmer for a further 1 minute. Taste and gradually add extra nam pla or lime juice, if needed. Remove and discard the lemon grass stalk.

Divide the vermicelli noodles among 4 bowls. Bring the soup back to the boil, then add to each bowl. The heat of the soup will warm the noodles. To garnish, sprinkle with coriander leaves.

SERVES 4

115 g/4 oz dried vermicelli noodles

1.2 litres/2 pints chicken or vegetable stock

1 lemon grass stalk, crushed

1-cm/$^{1}/_{2}$-inch piece fresh root ginger, peeled and very finely chopped

2 fresh kaffir lime leaves, thinly sliced

1 fresh red chilli, or to taste, deseeded and thinly sliced

2 skinless, boneless chicken breasts, thinly sliced

200 ml/7 fl oz coconut cream

2–3 tbsp nam pla (Thai fish sauce)

1–2 tbsp fresh lime juice

55 g/2 oz beansprouts

4 spring onions, green part only, finely sliced

fresh coriander leaves, to garnish

Duck with Spring Onion Soup

Slash the skin of the duck 3 or 4 times with a sharp knife and rub in the curry paste. Cook the duck breasts, skin-side down, in a wok or frying pan over a high heat for 2–3 minutes. Turn over, reduce the heat and cook for a further 3–4 minutes, until cooked through. Lift out and slice thickly. Set aside and keep warm.

Meanwhile, heat the oil in a wok or large frying pan and stir-fry half the spring onions, the garlic, ginger, carrots and red pepper for 2–3 minutes. Pour in the stock and add the chilli sauce, soy sauce and mushrooms. Bring to the boil, lower the heat and simmer for 4–5 minutes.

Ladle the soup into warmed bowls, top with the duck slices and garnish with the remaining spring onions. Serve immediately.

SERVES 4

2 duck breasts, skin on

2 tbsp red curry paste

2 tbsp vegetable or groundnut oil

bunch of spring onions, chopped

2 garlic cloves, crushed

5-cm/2-inch piece fresh root ginger, grated

2 carrots, thinly sliced

1 red pepper, deseeded and cut into strips

1 litre/$1^3/_4$ pints chicken stock

2 tbsp sweet chilli sauce

3–4 tbsp Thai soy sauce

400 g/14 oz canned straw mushrooms, drained

Pork Chilli Soup

Heat the oil in a large saucepan over a medium-high heat. Add the pork, season with salt and pepper, and cook until no longer pink, stirring frequently. Reduce the heat to medium and add the onion, celery, red pepper and garlic. Cover and continue cooking for 5 minutes, stirring occasionally, until the onion is softened.

Add the tomato purée, tomatoes and the stock. Add the coriander, cumin, oregano and chilli powder. Stir in the ingredients to combine well.

Bring just to the boil, reduce the heat to low, cover and simmer for 30–40 minutes until all the vegetables are very tender. Taste and adjust the seasoning, adding more chilli powder if you like it hotter.

Ladle the chilli into warmed bowls and sprinkle with coriander. Top each serving with a spoonful of soured cream and serve.

SERVES 4

2 tsp olive oil

500 g/1 lb 2 oz fresh lean pork mince

1 onion, finely chopped

1 celery stick, finely chopped

1 red pepper, cored, deseeded and finely chopped

2–3 garlic cloves, finely chopped

3 tbsp tomato purée

400 g/14 oz canned chopped tomatoes

450 ml/16 fl oz chicken stock

$1/8$ tsp ground coriander

$1/8$ tsp ground cumin

$1/4$ tsp dried oregano

1 tsp mild chilli powder, or to taste

salt and pepper

fresh coriander leaves, to garnish

soured cream, to serve

Sweetcorn & Smoked Chilli Soup

Heat the oil in a large, heavy-based saucepan. Add the onions and cook over a low heat, stirring occasionally, for 5 minutes, or until softened. Stir in the sweetcorn, cover and cook for a further 3 minutes.

Add the stock, half the milk, the chillies and garlic and season with salt. Bring to the boil, reduce the heat, then cover and simmer for 15–20 minutes.

Stir in the remaining milk. Reserve about 175 ml/6 fl oz of the soup solids. Transfer the remaining soup to a food processor or blender and process to a coarse purée.

Return the soup to the saucepan and stir in the reserved soup solids, the chorizo, lime juice and coriander. Reheat to simmering point, stirring constantly. Ladle into warmed bowls and serve immediately.

SERVES 4

1 tbsp sunflower oil

2 onions, chopped

550 g/1 lb 4 oz frozen sweetcorn kernels, thawed

600 ml/1 pint chicken stock

425 ml/15 fl oz milk

4 chipotle chillies, deseeded and finely chopped

2 garlic cloves, finely chopped

salt

55 g/2 oz chorizo sausage, thinly sliced

2 tbsp lime juice

2 tbsp chopped fresh coriander

Spicy Beef & Noodle Soup

Pour the stock into a large saucepan and bring to the boil. Meanwhile, heat the oil in a wok or large frying pan. Add a third of the noodles and fry for 10–20 seconds, until they have puffed up. Lift out with tongs, drain on kitchen paper and set aside. Discard all but 2 tablespoons of the oil.

Add the shallots, garlic and ginger to the wok or frying pan and stir-fry for 1 minute. Add the beef and curry paste and stir-fry for a further 3–4 minutes, until tender.

Add the beef mixture, the uncooked noodles, soy sauce and fish sauce to the saucepan of stock and simmer for 2–3 minutes, until the noodles have swelled. Serve hot garnished with the chopped coriander and the reserved crispy noodles.

SERVES 4

1 litre/1^3/$_4$ pints beef stock

150 ml/5 fl oz vegetable or groundnut oil

85 g/3 oz rice vermicelli noodles

2 shallots, thinly sliced

2 garlic cloves, crushed

2.5-cm/1-inch piece fresh root ginger, thinly sliced

225-g/8-oz piece fillet steak, cut into thin strips

2 tbsp green curry paste

2 tbsp Thai soy sauce

1 tbsp fish sauce

chopped fresh coriander, to garnish

Asian Lamb Soup

Trim all visible fat from the lamb and slice the meat thinly. Cut the slices into bite-sized pieces. Spread the meat in one layer on a plate and sprinkle over the garlic and 1 tablespoon of the soy sauce. Leave to marinate, covered, for at least 10 minutes or up to 1 hour.

Put the stock in a saucepan with the ginger, lemon grass, remaining soy sauce and the chilli purée. Bring just to the boil, reduce the heat, cover and simmer for 10–15 minutes.

When ready to serve the soup, place the tomatoes, spring onions, beansprouts and fresh coriander leaves into the simmering stock.

Heat the oil in a frying pan and add the lamb with its marinade. Stir-fry the lamb just until it is no longer red and divide among warmed bowls.

Ladle the hot stock over and serve immediately.

SERVES 4

150 g/5^1/$_2$ oz lean tender lamb, such as neck fillet or leg steak

2 garlic cloves, very finely chopped

2 tbsp soy sauce

1.2 litres/2 pints chicken stock

1 tbsp grated fresh root ginger

5-cm/2-inch piece lemon grass, sliced into very thin rounds

^{1}/$_4$ tsp chilli purée, or to taste

6–8 cherry tomatoes, quartered

4 spring onions, sliced finely

50 g/1^3/$_4$ oz beansprouts, snapped in half

2 tbsp fresh coriander leaves

1 tsp olive oil

Sweetcorn & Crab Soup

Heat the oil in a large frying pan and fry the garlic, shallots, lemon grass and ginger over a low heat, stirring occasionally, for 2–3 minutes, until softened. Add the stock and coconut milk and bring to the boil. Add the sweetcorn, lower the heat and simmer gently for 3–4 minutes.

Add the crabmeat, fish sauce, lime juice and sugar and simmer gently for 1 minute. Ladle into warmed bowls, garnish with the chopped coriander and serve immediately.

SERVES 6

2 tbsp vegetable or groundnut oil

4 garlic cloves, finely chopped

5 shallots, finely chopped

2 lemon grass stalks, finely chopped

2.5-cm/1-inch piece fresh root ginger, finely chopped

1 litre/$1^3/_4$ pints chicken stock

400 g/14 oz canned coconut milk

225 g/8 oz frozen sweetcorn kernels

350 g/12 oz canned crabmeat, drained and shredded

2 tbsp fish sauce

juice of 1 lime

1 tsp palm sugar or soft light brown sugar

bunch of fresh coriander, chopped, to garnish

Thai-Style Seafood Soup

Put the stock in a saucepan with the lemon grass, lime rind, ginger and chilli purée. Bring just to the boil, reduce the heat, cover and simmer for 10–15 minutes.

Cut the prawns almost in half lengthways, keeping the tail intact.

Strain the stock, return to the saucepan and bring to a simmer. Add the spring onion and cook for 2–3 minutes. Taste and season with salt, if needed, and stir in a little more chilli purée if wished.

Add the scallops and prawns and poach for about 1 minute until they turn opaque and the prawns curl.

Stir in the fresh coriander leaves, ladle the soup into warmed bowls, dividing the shellfish evenly, and garnish with chillies.

SERVES 4

1.2 litres/2 pints fish stock

1 lemon grass stalk, split lengthways

pared rind of $^{1}/_{2}$ lime, or 1 lime leaf

2.5-cm/1-inch piece fresh root
   ginger, sliced

$^{1}/_{4}$ tsp chilli purée, or to taste

200 g/7 oz large or medium raw
   prawns, peeled

4–6 spring onions, sliced

250 g/9 oz scallops

2 tbsp fresh coriander leaves

salt

finely chopped red chillies,
   to garnish